SELF-CARE
— FOR —
EVERY DAY

Simple Tips and Soothing Quotes
to Help You Feel Your Best

vie

INTRODUCTION

Self-care can sound like a big deal. We might imagine it as vacations, grooming routines or exercise regimes – things that are expensive or hard to incorporate into our lives. Perhaps we even think of it as selfish, something that takes up time we could be giving to our family, work or community.

But self-care simply means taking care of yourself. It doesn't have to cost lots of money or take up hours of your week. It is about small acts of love and kindness. And it's not just important, it's vital.

When we don't take care of ourselves, we feel depleted and sad. Neglecting ourselves can make it harder to help our loved ones, or thrive in our careers.

You may find it difficult to look after yourself, as many of us do, but this little book aims to help you introduce self-care practices into every day. Be open-minded and approach self-care with curiosity and gentleness – and see what comes from doing that. The results could be life-changing.

SMILE, BREATHE
AND GO SLOWLY.

Thích Nhất Hạnh

SELF-CARE IS NEVER A
SELFISH ACT — IT IS SIMPLY
GOOD STEWARDSHIP OF
THE ONLY GIFT I HAVE, THE
GIFT I WAS PUT ON EARTH
TO OFFER TO OTHERS.

Parker Palmer

LISTEN IN

Many of us are good at understanding the needs of our family, friends and the organizations we work for. But when it comes to working out how to look after ourselves, nourish our bodies or take care of our emotional needs, we can feel clueless. When we feel this way, the secret is to listen a little harder.

Real self-care is about noticing what you need. It might involve doing something you love or something you've always wanted to do, but it can also be about the not doing – taking rest or choosing to serve yourself as a priority. Make time to listen to your heart and create some mental space so you can figure out what you really need.

Dive deep and don't be afraid. Self-care can be magical! We all deserve to feel taken care of – it is perhaps the greatest kindness we can offer ourselves.

SELF-CARE IS SO MUCH MORE THAN A BEAUTY REGIMEN OR AN EXTERNAL THING YOU DO.

Carrie-Anne Moss

BRUSH YOUR TEETH

Sometimes it's the little things that count. If you are finding it hard to look after yourself, start with the minutiae: brushing your teeth, pouring yourself a large glass of water or putting on a jumper that makes you feel warm and cosy. These small acts of self-care set a positive intention – to look after yourself and meet your most basic human needs. Once you start to take care of the little things, bigger things can follow.

TO LOVE ONESELF IS
THE BEGINNING OF A
LIFELONG ROMANCE.

Oscar Wilde

SELF-LOVE HAS VERY
LITTLE TO DO WITH
HOW YOU FEEL ABOUT
YOUR OUTER SELF.
IT'S ABOUT ACCEPTING
ALL OF YOURSELF.

Tyra Banks

TALK TO YOURSELF KINDLY

We all have an inner voice, some of us an inner voice that can be critical and even unkind. While we often treat our friends with compassion, support their successes and buoy them up when they feel down, we are not always so caring toward ourselves. Look in the mirror and try saying something kind. If you find this difficult, be more specific. Remind yourself when you last did something thoughtful for somebody or smiled at a stranger. Remember all the things you are good at and the people who are happy to see you every day.

JUST WHEN YOU FEEL YOU
HAVE NO TIME TO RELAX,
KNOW THAT THIS IS THE
MOMENT YOU MOST NEED
TO MAKE TIME TO RELAX.

Matt Haig

THERE IS ONLY ONE
CORNER OF THE UNIVERSE
YOU CAN BE CERTAIN OF
IMPROVING, AND THAT'S
YOUR OWN SELF.

Aldous Huxley

MICRO-TIDYING

Clutter and mess can make us feel stressed and anxious. Worse still, sometimes it seems impossible to know where to start, or we feel that we'll never have the time or energy to sort everything out. A micro-tidy means choosing just one thing – a drawer, a shelf, a corner of the kitchen – to clean and organize. Clear the space, clean the surface and then put things back neatly, setting aside anything you no longer need for a charity shop or recycling.

TAKE YOURSELF OUT ON A DATE

Celebrate self-love by taking yourself out!
If you could plan a lovely day for yourself,
where would you go? A slow lunch in a
new cafe with a good book to read? Or is
there an exhibition or film you'd like to
see? What are your needs and desires?
If you were trying really hard to please
yourself, what would that involve?

Your plans don't have to cost anything
either. There are so many ways to

treat yourself that are totally free! You could pack a rucksack and take yourself on a hike or explore a new part of your town. Or you could spend the day lying in a park, listening to a playlist you love.

See this "date" as a chance to enjoy your own company and to follow your whims and desires. It might be the first time in a long while that you have put your needs before anybody else's. And if so, well done.

TAKE CARE OF YOUR INNER, SPIRITUAL BEAUTY. THAT WILL REFLECT IN YOUR FACE.

Dolores del Río

DO NOT BE AFRAID
TO GIVE YOURSELF
EVERYTHING YOU'VE
EVER WANTED IN LIFE.

Frank Lloyd Wright

FIND YOUR EXERCISE

Love it or lump it, the science is clear: exercise is good for us. We need to move our bodies in order to look after them, and exercise is as vital for our mental health as it is our physical. Fortunately, there are many ways to move, and there's no point forcing yourself to do a type of exercise that you dislike. There will always be people who love running but, if you don't enjoy it, try something different. Otherwise, you might end up being that person who tells themselves they really must go for a run, but never does, because you simply don't like running! Maybe you're someone who loves being outdoors and connecting with nature. In which case, the gym might not suit you, so try taking your exercise outdoors instead. If you are a sociable person, a group dance class might be more up your street than a solo hike. Be realistic and approach exercise with curiosity until you find the thing that works for you.

AND NOW THAT
YOU DON'T HAVE
TO BE PERFECT,
YOU CAN BE GOOD.

John Steinbeck

DON'T OVER-COMMIT

We often believe a full diary to be an
indicator of a successful life; it means
you have people to see, plenty of work
and multiple social engagements. But
sometimes this level of activity can be
overwhelming. Look at your diary and be
frank with yourself about whether you
need or want to be doing as much. Even if
you are someone who loves to make plans,
everyone needs space in their calendars
to either unwind and do nothing, or be
free to do something spontaneous.

HONESTLY, SELF-CARE
IS NOT FLUFFY – IT'S
SOMETHING WE SHOULD
TAKE SERIOUSLY.

Kris Carr

THIS REVOLUTIONARY ACT
OF TREATING OURSELVES
TENDERLY CAN BEGIN
TO UNDO THE AVERSIVE
MESSAGES OF A LIFETIME.

Tara Brach

BELLY BREATHING

Breathing into your belly has all sorts of amazing benefits. It encourages better oxygen flow around the body, reduces stress levels and relaxes the nervous system. And the best part: the effects are instantaneous.

So how do you do it? Start by getting really comfortable, either sitting or lying down. Place both hands on your belly, relax your shoulders and try to release any tension from around the jaw. As you inhale through your nose, breathe into your abdomen and allow it to expand like a balloon. As you exhale through your nose, allow everything to soften completely. Inhale and expand, then exhale, contract and soften. Practise repeating this several times.

Observe how you feel afterward. Next time you're feeling stressed, notice where you are breathing. If it's right up in your chest, try belly breathing to help you find your calm.

SURROUND YOURSELF
WITH PEOPLE, COLOUR,
SOUNDS AND WORK
THAT NOURISH YOU.

Susan Ariel Rainbow Kennedy

EVERY ONE OF US NEEDS
TO SHOW HOW MUCH WE
CARE FOR EACH OTHER
AND, IN THE PROCESS,
CARE FOR OURSELVES.

Diana, Princess of Wales

WALK AND TALK

Have you ever noticed how good it feels to chat to someone as you walk side by side? There's something about the rhythmic pattern of walking that is conducive to good conversation. Next time you want to talk to someone, why not arrange to do it over a stroll? Or, if you're feeling adventurous, chat while you trek up a hill! You might find the conversation flows more easily, and you'll be looking after both mind and body at the same time. A self-care double whammy!

YESTERDAY I WAS
CLEVER, SO I WANTED
TO CHANGE THE WORLD.
TODAY I AM WISE, SO I
AM CHANGING MYSELF.

Rumi

REACH OUT
TO A FRIEND

We all have people in our lives whose company we thrive on. People who support us and make us feel good about ourselves, who we can talk to about the things that matter. These individuals are integral to our wellness and happiness, yet sometimes it can be easy to go for weeks (or even months) without connecting. Reaching out to them can remind us that we are lucky to have their friendship and love, and gives us an opportunity to thank them for it. So make that call, set up a coffee date or plan a trip together.

LOVING YOURSELF
ISN'T VANITY.
IT'S SANITY.

Katrina Mayer

SING YOUR HEART OUT

There is so much joy to be found in singing your heart out whether your voice is high, low, in tune or has its own tune! We all have music and songs that we love, and it can be uplifting to sing – loudly and proudly – without restraint. Let it all go by singing along to the car radio, dancing and singing in the garden or doing karaoke with friends. Or, if you're looking for a new hobby, why not join a community choir?

WHEN I AM CONSTANTLY
RUNNING THERE IS NO TIME
FOR BEING. WHEN THERE IS
NO TIME FOR BEING THERE
IS NO TIME FOR LISTENING.

Madeleine L'Engle

TAKE YOUR TEA OUTSIDE

Hands up if you start your day with a cup of tea or coffee... But once you've made your drink, what do you do next? Instead of rushing to get on with your work or chores, take a few minutes to step outside and feel the fresh air and (if you're lucky) the sun on your face. Be present for a moment. Take a few deep breaths and pay attention to the sounds outside – from birds, to chatter, to traffic. Savour the small pleasure of a hot drink on a new day.

It can be easy to gulp down a coffee without noticing the taste or the temperature. We jump straight into our day without remembering to check in on ourselves. Just taking these extra few moments can be a really valuable way to start the morning – you'll feel more present and connected to yourself for it.

WOMEN NEED SOLITUDE
IN ORDER TO FIND AGAIN
THE TRUE ESSENCE
OF THEMSELVES.

Anne Morrow Lindbergh

ELEVATE YOUR EVENING

Elevating the everyday is a way of making life feel a little bit more special, and allows us to find joy in humdrum things. Often we eat dinner in front of the TV instead of conversing with company or really savouring our food. Why not make what could be a boring mid-week meal into something special? Set the table, maybe even bring out a tablecloth, light some candles and turn the lights down low. Put on some good music, use your best glasses and spice up your evening!

JOURNAL INTO THE DEEP

There are many different ways to approach journaling, whether it is simply recounting your day, listing things you are grateful for or using journaling prompts. But sometimes a structure can be limiting. Try regarding journaling as more of a brain dump – Julia Cameron came up with a technique called "morning pages" (where you produce three pages of longhand, stream-of-consciousness writing every morning) in her popular book *The Artist's Way*. Write freely about whatever you want – your day, the weather, the shopping list, etc. Once we clear out our admin and to-do lists, we often find ideas and inspiration hiding beneath.

YOU HAVE BEEN CRITICIZING
YOURSELF FOR YEARS AND
IT HASN'T WORKED. TRY
APPROVING OF YOURSELF
AND SEE WHAT HAPPENS.

Louise L. Hay

SHOW YOUR FEET SOME LOVE

Our feet take us everywhere we need to go yet they are often underappreciated. Showing them some gratitude is a little act of tenderness that they will appreciate. You could give them a soak in a washing-up bowl full of warm water or massage them gently before you go to bed. Or try rolling your feet backwards and forwards on a tennis ball – do this when seated comfortably with a long straight spine. This movement gently stretches the plantar fascia (a band of tissue on the bottom of the foot) and releases tension.

KEEP GOOD COMPANY,
READ GOOD BOOKS,
LOVE GOOD THINGS AND
CULTIVATE SOUL AND
BODY AS FAITHFULLY
AS YOU CAN.

Louisa May Alcott

THE IRONY IS THAT
WHEN WE TAKE CARE OF
OURSELVES FIRST, WE
ARE IN A MUCH STRONGER
PLACE TO TAKE CARE
OF THOSE WE LOVE.

Kate Hudson

CARING FOR MYSELF IS
NOT SELF-INDULGENCE,
IT IS SELF-PRESERVATION.

Audre Lorde

THE KETTLE STRETCH

How many times a day do you switch the kettle on and then immediately pick up your phone? Instead of checking your notifications as you wait for the water to boil, spend that minute checking in with your body. Are any areas in need of some attention? You could try inhaling, lifting your arms up high and sighing out loud as you lower them again. Or hold onto a worktop and shift your hips from side to side. Another thing you could give a go is drawing some gentle circles with your chin to ease tension in your neck. Your body will thank you for it.

WHEN I'M RESTED,
I'M AT MY BEST.

Halle Berry

IF YOUR COMPASSION
DOES NOT INCLUDE
YOURSELF, IT IS
INCOMPLETE.

Jack Kornfield

WALK WITH AWARENESS

Are you guilty of walking from A to B
without noticing anything around you?
Perhaps you walk and talk on your phone
at the same time or listen to music or
podcasts? While this can feel efficient,
there are huge mental benefits to
be found from simply observing your
surroundings. What can you see and hear?
What is new in your neighbourhood? What
seasonal changes have happened since you
last walked this route? The act of noticing
sights, sounds and smells is a form of
meditation, keeping you absolutely in the
moment and helping to calm a busy mind.

SPENDING AUDIT

This one might not sound like much fun, but it's often the jobs we never face up to that stress us out the most. Spending a morning examining your outgoings is a way to take control of your finances. This can be helpful if you're trying to save up for something, and is often really empowering. Make a warm drink, sit down with a spreadsheet or notebook, and get to grips with it all. List all your expenses, all the things you are saving up for and all the one-off costs as well as regular ones. This is one of those jobs that takes a bit of time, but the hardest part is actually deciding to get on with it. When you've finished and have the facts to hand, you may feel a sense of relief. Whatever happens, you'll be armed with the knowledge to take the next steps.

IT'S NOT SELFISH TO
LOVE YOURSELF... AND
MAKE YOUR HAPPINESS A
PRIORITY. IT'S NECESSARY.

Mandy Hale

LIFE SHOULD BE
TOUCHED, NOT STRANGLED.
YOU'VE GOT TO RELAX,
LET IT HAPPEN AT TIMES,
AND AT OTHERS MOVE
FORWARD WITH IT.

Ray Bradbury

I ALWAYS GIVE MYSELF
SUNDAYS AS A SPIRITUAL
BASE OF RENEWAL...
I ALLOW MYSELF TIME
TO BE — CAPITAL B-E
— WITH MYSELF.

Oprah Winfrey

TALK TO YOURSELF
LIKE YOU WOULD TO
SOMEONE YOU LOVE.

Brené Brown

MOVE SLOWLY

When we feel stressed people often advise us to slow down or take it easy, yet it can seem unhelpful and counter-intuitive to do so. But those mornings when you are racing around feeling fraught are always the ones when you end up spilling toothpaste down your top. Why not try to (very literally) move more slowly? Instead of running around to grab your possessions or tie your shoelaces while standing on one leg, actively try to move slowly and mindfully around the house. The effect can be surprisingly calming, and you may find you actually accomplish more!

ADOPT THE PACE OF
NATURE: HER SECRET
IS PATIENCE.

Ralph Waldo Emerson

MAKE AN INSPIRATION BOARD

It feels good to be reminded of the things we love or that support our creativity. While we could simply list them down, a pictorial reminder can be even more powerful.

One way to do this is to create an inspiration board of images to keep on a desk or pin up in the kitchen.

There are no rules so feel free to be as creative as you like! Start with a pinboard or a square of cardboard that you could cover in fabric, or use washi tape and stick things directly onto the wall.

Try gathering up postcards, magazine cut-outs or photographs you like. Find inspiring quotes from people you admire and write them out, or you could add notes from family and friends. Make it a little piece of you and the things you love.

REFLECT UPON YOUR PRESENT BLESSINGS — OF WHICH EVERY MAN HAS MANY — NOT ON YOUR PAST MISFORTUNES, OF WHICH ALL MEN HAVE SOME.

Charles Dickens

LIMIT NEWS CONSUMPTION

Do you find yourself glued to the newsfeed on your phone? It's an easy thing to do, but spending hours consuming news can be draining and leave us feeling helpless. It might be a good idea to set a time limit for how long you spend reading the news. You could also try to look at "good news" websites and magazines to remind yourself that although the world can be a challenging place, it is also full of acts of kindness and generosity.

SELF-CARE MEANS
GIVING YOURSELF
PERMISSION TO PAUSE.

Cecilia Tran

WHEN YOU RECOVER OR
DISCOVER SOMETHING THAT
NOURISHES YOUR SOUL AND
BRINGS JOY, CARE ENOUGH
ABOUT YOURSELF TO MAKE
ROOM FOR IT IN YOUR LIFE.

Jean Shinoda Bolen

LOVE YOURSELF FIRST
AND EVERYTHING ELSE
FALLS IN LINE. YOU REALLY
HAVE TO LOVE YOURSELF
TO GET ANYTHING
DONE IN THIS WORLD.

Lucille Ball

SELF-CARE IS
HOW YOU TAKE
YOUR POWER BACK.

Lalah Delia

WARRIOR STRETCHES

There are so many yoga postures and sequences out there and, as all our bodies are different, we won't all feel the same way in any one pose. But there are positions that have certain qualities to them – restful, energizing, powerful – and the warrior poses inspire exactly the sort of feelings you'd expect. So next time you need a boost in confidence, perhaps before a big meeting or when something takes you out of your comfort zone, try taking a few breaths in Warrior II. Stand in a wide stance with your feet parallel to each other, turn one foot out to the side and turn your head to the same side. Bend your front knee so it is stacked above your ankle. Lift your arms to the side to shoulder height, aligning them directly over your legs. With your palms facing down, take your gaze over your leading hand. Take full deep breaths into your belly, keeping your legs strong. Feel your power. After ten seconds, or as long as you feel comfortable, try the pose on the other side.

LOVE YOURSELF ENOUGH
TO SET BOUNDARIES. YOUR
TIME AND ENERGY ARE
PRECIOUS. YOU GET TO
CHOOSE HOW YOU USE IT.

Anna Taylor

ALMOST EVERYTHING
WILL WORK AGAIN IF
YOU UNPLUG IT FOR A FEW
MINUTES, INCLUDING YOU.

Anne Lamott

KITCHEN DANCE PARTY

Can't go out to a party? Bring the dancing to your house! A kitchen dance party is a sure way to boost energy and raise your mood. Lose your inhibitions by cutting shapes and striking a pose. Whether your choice is dad dancing, mum dancing or break dancing, all styles go in the kitchen! You could even try dimming the lights and drumming on the pots and pans to really get the party started.

IF YOU HAVE THE
ABILITY TO LOVE,
LOVE YOURSELF FIRST.

Charles Bukowski

STAY HYDRATED

Water is free, easily available and vital for good health, yet lots of us don't actually drink enough of it. Make a promise to yourself to prioritize your hydration – one of the most basic but essential forms of self-care. Remember your water bottle, swap out caffeine for herbal teas, or infuse a jug of water with cucumber, lemon, celery or mint – whatever it takes to make sure you get around 2 litres, or six to eight glasses, of water a day into your system.

PLANT A SEED

Have you ever witnessed the joy of a toddler planting a tiny sunflower seed and watching it transform into a giant flower? Gardening can seem like magic, but perhaps its greatest pleasure comes from the fact that it takes only a short while to receive the fruits of your labour. Why not try planting your own seeds, whether it's flowers for the house or vegetables to nourish your body? All it takes is a packet of seeds, a sunny windowsill and a little patience.

LET SOMETHING GO

We can all carry emotional baggage with us, which often really weighs us down. We can hold onto old arguments, hurtful things that people have said to us, things that we never said or ways we have behaved that we regret. Holding onto it all is exhausting. What would happen if you decided to release some of it? Or forgive yourself for a mistake? The best thing you can do is learn from the past and let it go.

IT IS SO IMPORTANT TO
TAKE TIME FOR YOURSELF
AND FIND CLARITY.
THE MOST IMPORTANT
RELATIONSHIP IS THE ONE
YOU HAVE WITH YOURSELF.

Diane von Fürstenberg

HAVE AN APP CLEAR-OUT

Smartphone technology means we are more distracted than ever. Every day we are interrupted by alerts popping up: emails vibrating during mealtimes and multiple group chats filling our phones with hundreds of messages. It can be exhausting to keep up with it all, and it's no wonder that many of us struggle to concentrate when our attention is constantly being pulled in different directions.

Try noticing how these distractions make you feel. When your smartphone alerts you to yet another thing, who or what is losing out on your attention? Maybe it's time to remove some of these distractions. Next time you have a few minutes spare, try doing an audit of your phone. Could you delete a few apps, or exit group chats that no longer serve you? Could you set time limits on the apps you would like to continue using? Making a few changes like this will allow you to reclaim a little time and focus for the things that really matter to you.

PRACTISE SELF-RESCUE
FIRST BEFORE YOU
"HELP" SOMEONE ELSE.

Maureen Joyce Connolly

SEE YOUR DOCTOR

There are all sorts of reasons we avoid going to the doctor, whether we feel we don't have time or that our concerns are too trivial. But if we had a friend with a health worry, we would probably advise them to make the trip to the surgery. Try to treat yourself with the same love and respect, and make sure you schedule an appointment to discuss any physical or mental concerns with your doctor. Having a conversation might be enough to alleviate anxiety, and if not, you will have sought out the help you need and deserve.

STROKE A PET

There's a reason why dogs are brought into hospitals to visit patients – they help us feel better. Just looking at a happy dog in the park (or even a meme of one online) can often be enough to make us smile. Spending time with animals also has huge therapeutic benefits. The company of pets is proven to help with anxiety and stress, and the very act of stroking the fur of an animal can reduce the stress hormone cortisol. So, next time you feel upset, reach out for your pet.

THE MOST CREATIVE
ACT YOU WILL EVER
UNDERTAKE IS THE ACT
OF CREATING YOURSELF.

Deepak Chopra

THERE ARE DAYS I DROP
WORDS OF COMFORT ON
MYSELF LIKE FALLING
LEAVES AND REMEMBER
THAT IT IS ENOUGH TO BE
TAKEN CARE OF BY MYSELF.

Brian Andreas

YOUR BRAIN IS LIKE A
COMPUTER, YOU HAVE
TO REFRESH OR IT'S
GOING TO CRASH.

Missy Elliott

MAKE A WISH

It might sound corny, but it can feel good to make a wish! We all have hopes, dreams and aspirations that making a wish can help us realize. While you might not believe in the art of manifestation, just saying out loud or writing down a wish or desire does take you one step closer to achieving it. Write a wish on a piece of paper and keep it inside your wallet as a reminder of your goal and to keep you on track. Have some self-belief and know that you deserve for your wishes to come true.

SELF-COMPASSION
IS SIMPLY GIVING THE
SAME KINDNESS TO
OURSELVES THAT WE
WOULD GIVE TO OTHERS.

Christopher Germer

USE A MANTRA

In Eastern spiritual practices, a "mantra" is a sacred word that is often repeated and is thought to have a special power. Using a mantra as part of your meditation practice can help to focus the mind, silence inner chatter and calm the nervous system.

Mantras were traditionally Sanskrit words, such as "om" (thought to be the sound of the universe) and "soham" (which translates to "I am that"). In the western world, we can also use words or short phrases that are significant or helpful to us, such as "I am enough", "I can do it", "keep breathing" or something else totally personal to you.

See if you can find a phrase that resonates with you and try whispering it to yourself as part of your meditation practice. Practise this for a few minutes each day and notice how your mantra makes you feel.

ONE OF THE GREATEST
REGRETS IN LIFE IS BEING
WHAT OTHERS WOULD
WANT YOU TO BE, RATHER
THAN BEING YOURSELF.

Shannon L. Alder

SELF-CARE IS NOT A WASTE OF TIME; SELF-CARE MAKES YOUR USE OF TIME MORE SUSTAINABLE.

Jackie Viramontez

DOODLING FOR RELAXATION

Doodling can be very soothing. The joy of this drawing method is that there is no plan whatsoever as to where your picture is going. It's scribbling just for the sake of it. Grab whatever paper you've got to hand – an envelope, leaflet or notebook – and just start drawing. If you need a starting point, pick a shape like a circle, a heart or spiral and work outward from there. Be playful, experimental and free, and see where it takes you!

I REMIND MYSELF TO BE KIND TO MYSELF, AND AS SLIGHTLY RIDICULOUS AS IT MAY SOUND, TO TREAT MYSELF IN THE SAME GENTLE WAY I'D WANT TO TREAT A DAUGHTER OF MINE.

Emma Stone

THE TIME TO RELAX
IS WHEN YOU DON'T
HAVE TIME FOR IT.

Sydney J. Harris

OUR BODIES ARE OUR
GARDENS, TO THE
WHICH OUR WILLS
ARE GARDENERS.

William Shakespeare

GET DRESSED UP

What you wear and how you present yourself can change the way you feel. If you are someone who tends to only make an effort for special occasions, why not try getting all dressed up for something mundane – to walk the dog, do the school run or go to the supermarket. Make an effort simply for yourself and for the joy of dressing up. Perhaps you'll walk taller or be more inclined to engage with strangers. It might even make you feel a bit better about yourself.

BEAUTY BEGINS THE
MOMENT YOU DECIDE
TO BE YOURSELF.

Coco Chanel

FIND YOUR COMMUNITY

Isolation and loneliness can be a huge problem, not just for the elderly but for people at any stage in their lives. As humans we are social beings who thrive in communities, especially ones where we meet like-minded people or people from other walks of life who bring their own experiences and advice to the room.

If you feel that you lack a community, remember that it could be found in many different places. Some people discover theirs by following their spirituality – whether that's their religion or a practice like yoga or meditation. If this isn't for you, think about your interests and seek out people who share them. Do you have skills to contribute? Could you get involved with a local charity, help organize an event in your neighbourhood, join a choir or book club? Your people are out there – it's just a case of finding them.

I WANT TO FEEL MY
LIFE WHILE I'M IN IT.

Meryl Streep

SUNLIGHT FIRST THING

Research has shown that getting sunlight on your skin early in the morning can help you sleep better at night. The morning light helps to set our body's internal clock – and not going outside until midday can mess with that. Try getting out early for a week and see if it makes any difference to your sleep. At the very least, you can enjoy being up and about before the rest of the world!

WITHIN YOU, THERE IS
A STILLNESS AND A
SANCTUARY TO WHICH
YOU CAN RETREAT AT ANY
TIME AND BE YOURSELF.

Hermann Hesse

IF YOU CAN'T LOVE
YOURSELF, HOW IN THE
HELL YOU GONNA LOVE
SOMEBODY ELSE?

RuPaul

LISTEN TO A PODCAST

Whether your passions are in writing, gardening, activism, Pilates or literally anything else ever, there's a podcast for you. The wonderful thing is that you can listen to a podcast pretty much anywhere (often when you are doing something less enjoyable such as commuting, washing up or cleaning the bathroom). Search by topic or person and you might be amazed by what you find – perhaps an inspiring conversation between two people who fascinate you or some advice or encouragement to feed the soul.

YOU FIND PEACE NOT
BY REARRANGING THE
CIRCUMSTANCES OF YOUR
LIFE, BUT BY REALIZING
WHO YOU ARE AT THE
DEEPEST LEVEL.

Eckhart Tolle

STARGAZING FOR WELL-BEING

On a clear night when the stars are out, it can feel pretty incredible to gaze up and wonder at the magnitude of the universe. Just pondering the stars and planets above is enough to make us feel like part of a big, complicated universe. Sometimes we can feel very detached from the world around us, but an evening spent under the stars might be enough to remind us that we are all made up of the same stuff, connected to each other and to the world around us. It is also a beautiful way to access the calming powers of the great outdoors.

THE POWER OF SHARING

The phrase "sharing is caring" is often directed at young children, but, in a world where we have a huge problem with wastage, it could be better applied to adults. Sharing can help us look after the planet and those around us. Consider borrowing a dress for a party rather than buying a new one, or lending the garden and electrical equipment you have in the shed to someone who could make good use of it. Sharing your possessions in your local community could also help you better connect with those around you.

CHECK IN WITH YOURSELF

You may well have a weekly or even daily meeting to check in with your team or boss at work, but have you ever thought about having a check-in with yourself? Could you improve your week by examining the previous one and celebrating your triumphs or reminding yourself of the things you might like to approach differently? A personal weekly check-in could take whatever form you like. It might just be about your work, but it could also be really helpful to look holistically at all areas of your life, whether it's relationships, fitness or mental health.

During the meeting you could set yourself a plan for the week ahead. You could re-examine goals, set to-do lists or simply look through all the things you managed to achieve and give yourself a pat on the back. Reward your hard work by scheduling in a long lunchtime walk, or notice when you've been feeling disconnected and diarize that coffee with a friend.

SELF-CARE IS THE
NON-NEGOTIABLE.
THAT'S THE THING
THAT YOU HAVE TO DO.

Jonathan Van Ness

SELF-CARE EQUALS
SUCCESS. YOU'RE GOING
TO BE MORE SUCCESSFUL
IF YOU TAKE CARE
OF YOURSELF AND
YOU'RE HEALTHY.

Beth Behrs

WRITE A THANK YOU NOTE

A handwritten thank you note is a joy to receive. It makes us feel so much more special than a text or an email. But it can feel as good to do the thanking as it does to be thanked! Who could you write a thank you note to? It doesn't need to be for anything grand, perhaps just the cup of coffee someone invited you for or some garden produce you were given by a neighbour. Enjoy writing your note on beautiful paper or a postcard while you remember and celebrate the person and occasion for which you are thankful.

THE CHALLENGE IS
NOT TO BE PERFECT,
IT'S TO BE WHOLE.

Jane Fonda

BUY YOURSELF A BEAUTY TREAT

While it's true that there's more to self-care than a day at the spa, it can still feel nice to treat yourself to some new moisturizer, nail polish, bubble bath or anything that allows you to pamper yourself. The value is in the intention as well as the product itself. You could set yourself a budget – it doesn't have to be much – and choose just one item that will make you feel special.

BREATHE. LET GO.
AND REMIND YOURSELF
THAT THIS VERY MOMENT
IS THE ONLY ONE YOU
KNOW YOU HAVE FOR SURE.

Oprah Winfrey

BEAUTY IS HOW YOU FEEL
INSIDE, AND IT REFLECTS
IN YOUR EYES. IT IS NOT
SOMETHING PHYSICAL.

Sophia Loren

ONE PERSON'S SELF-
CARE ISN'T NECESSARILY
ANOTHER'S — THERE
IS GOING TO BE A LOT
OF INDIVIDUALITY.

Gail Saltz

ENJOY MAKING PLANS

We all know that a holiday or day trip can make us feel great, but have you ever thought about the psychological benefits of the planning process? The act of organizing a trip and looking forward to it can make us feel uplifted and excited. The other great news is that, in some ways, it is the gift that keeps on giving. When we talk about it afterward with friends or look through our photos, we continue to feel happy and reap the benefits of the experience.

TRAVEL AND CHANGE
OF PLACE IMPART NEW
VIGOUR TO THE MIND.

Seneca

ASK FOR HELP

When was the last time you reached out to someone and asked for help? Sometimes we can struggle to start the conversation, but if a friend asked you for practical help or a listening ear, you would probably jump to their aid. Think about areas of your life where you are struggling. Is there someone who could help? It might be with childcare or a DIY task you can't manage alone, or maybe you need some specialist advice from a friend or even a professional. Don't be afraid to reach out, or contact a doctor or mental health charity if you need to.

SELF-LOVE IS
THE SOURCE OF ALL
OUR OTHER LOVES.

Pierre Corneille

HABIT TRACK

If you are trying to incorporate several elements of self-care into your daily or weekly life, it might be a good idea to make a habit tracker. This is simply a chart showing the habit, for example "drink more water", and the days of the week. You could make a grid in your diary or planner and tick off the days where you manage to achieve that element of self-care. It's a way to be accountable but it is also a way to celebrate your kindnesses to yourself.

SLOW-COOK SOMETHING

It can be easy to get into a pattern of cooking or eating the same food every week. A little variety can be a good thing and, if it is cooked with love and patience, so much the better. Why not raid the recipe books or look online for a one-pot, slow-cook recipe for a hearty, comforting supper? If it's something you can make earlier in the day and leave cooking slowly, you'll be welcomed home to the delicious aroma of home cooking, and your dinner waiting. What could be nicer?

WE CAN CLIMB
MOUNTAINS WITH
SELF-LOVE.

Samira Wiley

WE CANNOT DIRECT
THE WIND, BUT WE
CAN ADJUST THE SAILS.

Anonymous

FIND YOUR FLOW STATE

We often hear people talking about finding their "flow state", which means being totally absorbed or immersed in an activity. It sounds easy but many of us find it very challenging to be truly present in a task. We can't concentrate or enjoy what we are doing because our mind is elsewhere.

Try to identify a task that you could lose yourself in, whether it is something mundane like raking up leaves, or something more adventurous like climbing a hill. You could simply turn your attention to something you'd already planned to do and make an effort to be fully present in it. It could be an afternoon reading a new novel or listening to a podcast without your mind wandering elsewhere. You'll know when you've found that "flow state" as you won't feel bored or distracted and time will pass without you noticing.

ABOVE ALL, BE THE HEROINE OF YOUR LIFE.

Nora Ephron

KNOW YOUR WARNING SIGNS

In order to look after our mental well-being, we need to recognize our own signs of stress and anxiety. These can often present themselves as physical sensations. For example, if someone is saying something that makes you feel vulnerable or unsettled, you might feel a tightening in your chest or throat, or perhaps have a desire to wrap your arms around yourself in protection. Get to know your signs so you can pause, take a deep breath and then respond with kindness and compassion toward yourself. If you regularly experience physical symptoms of stress or anxiety, seek help from a professional.

WE TURN NOT OLDER
WITH YEARS BUT
NEWER EVERY DAY.

Emily Dickinson

TAKE CARE OF YOUR BODY.
IT'S THE ONLY PLACE
YOU HAVE TO LIVE.

Jim Rohn

MAKE A GRATITUDE JAR

It can be easy to take both big and small things for granted, so acknowledging the goodness in our lives is a valuable process. You could write a daily or weekly gratitude list, naming the things you are grateful for, be it health, a favourite TV show or a close friend. But it's also fun making a gratitude jar and filling it with scraps of paper detailing the things that bring you joy. When you are feeling blue, just grab the jar and reach inside it for a reminder of all the good you have in your life.

SOLVE A PUZZLE

We often think about how we can best take care of our physical bodies, but how good are you at looking after your brain? A recent study in the International Journal of Psychiatric Psychology found that engaging regularly in number puzzles has a positive effect on cognitive function. If puzzles can improve the health of our brain, it might be wise to fill in that sudoku from the paper or find a puzzle app to download onto your phone. Perhaps next time you need to split a bill in a restaurant or tot up some expenses, do the sum in your head instead of reaching for the calculator app.

SELF-CARE MEANS
CONSIDERING YOURSELF A
WORTHWHILE PERSON AND
PRESENTING YOURSELF
AS VALUABLE, CAPABLE,
AND DESERVING.

Arin Murphy-Hiscock

WHEN YOU SAY "YES"
TO OTHERS MAKE SURE
YOU ARE NOT SAYING
"NO" TO YOURSELF.

Paulo Coelho

HUG SOMEONE YOU LOVE

Studies have shown that giving someone a hug can reduce stress for both you and the person you're hugging – a great reason to cuddle your loved ones when you can. Touch is incredibly important to us as humans and, without it, we can feel lonely and isolated. When we are down (and when we are up) nothing beats a big bear hug from someone you love. So give a hug or ask for one, and remember what it feels like to be squeezed by a good friend.

OWNING OUR STORY
AND LOVING OURSELVES
THROUGH THAT PROCESS
IS THE BRAVEST THING
WE'LL EVER DO.

Brené Brown

SPEND TIME WITH TREES

You might have heard the term "forest bathing", a.k.a. the Japanese art of relaxing among the trees. The idea is that simply walking, breathing and being in the midst of trees is good for body and soul. If this sounds appealing, a trip to the trees could be just what you need to pick yourself up.

Find a wood, forest or park and spend some time walking around and observing the trees. Breathe deeply and notice the smell of the leaves or touch their bark. Be curious. How many times have you walked past a tree and failed to take in a single detail about it?

See if you can start to recognize trees at different times of the year, with or without their foliage. Ancient trees are particularly special – there is something awe-inspiring about being in the presence of a tree that has silently witnessed the last hundred years or so.

THE PERFECT MAN OF OLD
LOOKED AFTER HIMSELF
FIRST BEFORE LOOKING
TO HELP OTHERS.

Zhuangzi

LIGHTEN UP ON YOURSELF. NO ONE IS PERFECT. GENTLY ACCEPT YOUR HUMANNESS.

Deborah Day

READ A GOOD BOOK

Curling up with a good book has to be one of the simplest and most enjoyable pleasures in life. In a world full of demanding technology, reading a physical book feels like the ultimate low-key activity. Why not ask a friend to lend you their latest good read? Or visit a second-hand bookshop or your local library and enjoy the process of browsing and choosing something that sounds enticing. Then sit down and snuggle up!

UNTIL YOU VALUE
YOURSELF, YOU WON'T
VALUE YOUR TIME.
UNTIL YOU VALUE YOUR
TIME, YOU WILL NOT DO
ANYTHING WITH IT.

M. Scott Peck

CANDLE MEDITATION

Candle meditation or candle gazing is an ancient practice which involves sitting and staring at the flickering flame of a candle. It sounds easy, and in some ways it is, but in a world where we are more distracted than ever, it can be challenging to sit still. By watching the flame dancing and moving, we can improve our focus and calm the mind.

It's simple to do. Find a quiet space and light a candle. Placing it at eye level will stop you from arching your neck. Start by watching the candle for a minute, seeing if you can stay focused. Thoughts will pop up, but try to acknowledge them and allow them to pass as you return your attention to the flame. In time, see if you can gradually increase the amount of time that you are practising. How do you feel afterwards?

SELF-CARE SHOULD
INCLUDE THE COLD
SHOWER AS WELL AS
THE SCENTED TUB.

Mary Catherine Bateson

SELF-LOVE, MY LIEGE,
IS NOT SO VILE A SIN,
AS SELF-NEGLECTING.

William Shakespeare

AN HOUR FOR YOU

We can find it very hard to make time for the things we love. Work, parenting or household admin can crowd out our passions. When we do get some rare time to ourselves, we often find it difficult to choose what to do with those precious minutes.

Next time you have an hour free, ring-fence it for something that you would love to do. The key to this exercise is to make sure you absolutely do not do what you think you *should* be doing (admin, housework, emails, etc)! Try to choose something you really want to do.

You could paint, write, sleep, practise yoga – whatever it is that you desire. And if you feel that inevitable indecision, try not to put too much pressure on yourself. It's just an hour after all! Go with what might be fun, inspiring or allow your heart to lift a little.

CARVE OUT AND CLAIM
THE TIME TO CARE FOR
YOURSELF AND KINDLE
YOUR OWN FIRE.

Amy Ippoliti

EMBRACE SILENCE

The world can be a very noisy place, and we often add to this noise with TV, music, radios and phones. How are we supposed to think clearly with our auditory attention being pulled in so many different directions? Try committing to an hour of silence, switching off your phone, turning off the music and deciding not to talk to anyone during that time. Think of it as a miniature silence retreat. Afterward, ask yourself whether you enjoyed it and assess if you feel calmer.

TAKE REST; A FIELD
THAT HAS RESTED GIVES
A BOUNTIFUL CROP.

Ovid

BE YOU, LOVE YOU.
ALL WAYS, ALWAYS.

Alexandra Elle

ADOPT A BEDTIME ROUTINE

We are often interested in other people's morning routines, be it early workouts, mindfulness practices, smoothie recipes or daily planning. A good morning regime can set you up well for the day ahead. It also sets an intention about what you want your day to look and feel like. But have you considered planning a bedtime routine? Winding down effectively and really preparing yourself for rest could help you sleep better, and that can only be a good thing!

There are plenty of things you could include: perhaps a few minutes of yoga, writing in a gratitude diary, spritzing an aromatherapy sleep spray on your pillow or a daily tidy of your bedside table. Just taking a few little steps like this can cue your body for sleep and hopefully give you the gift of a peaceful and rejuvenating slumber.

PUT YOUR
PHONE TO BED

To give yourself the best chance of a good night's sleep, try avoiding screens and late-night scrolling. Blue light interferes with our body's production of the sleep hormone melatonin, and replying to messages late at night can be distracting and not conducive to good rest. Having a "screen switch-off time" an hour or so before you go to bed is a way to help you prepare for sleep. You could go even further and make the bedroom a screen-free zone or allocate a drawer or box downstairs to put your phone inside each night.

HAPPINESS DOESN'T
DEPEND ON OUTWARD
CONDITIONS. IT DEPENDS
ON INNER CONDITIONS.

Dale Carnegie

Self-Kindness

Claire Chamberlain

Hardback

ISBN: 978-1-80007-440-8

Learn a radical new approach to self-love with this beautiful handbook. Whether you're at the beginning of your journey to self-acceptance, or you're a seasoned self-love advocate, *Self-Kindness* will help you to deepen your self-love and grow your happiness through a combination of practical tips and actionable advice.